Poetry Still Exists and So Do I

Written by: Jessica Ann
(Her First Book)

ISBN 978-1-63961-765-4 (paperback)
ISBN 978-1-63961-766-1 (digital)

Copyright © 2024 by Jessica Ann

All rights reserved. No part of this publication may be reproduced, distributed, or transmitted in any form or by any means, including photocopying, recording, or other electronic or mechanical methods without the prior written permission of the publisher. For permission requests, solicit the publisher via the address below.

Christian Faith Publishing
832 Park Avenue
Meadville, PA 16335
www.christianfaithpublishing.com

Printed in the United States of America

I am doing my best to live with DiGeorge Syndrome,
My Family, God and Everybody Else.
I push through the pain by giving
it a voice we call poetry.

Dear Pain

Yes again—I'm talking to you
Everything to my body
I feel it and see
you do
Should I sit awake with you
Should I instead
try going to bed
Doesn't matter what all I do
So heavily you tread
marching on ahead
It's all in my head
They always say
If I should hope to fall asleep
when all night
It's you I fight
Because you never go away
You stay
all day long
But I'm strong
I power through
I am tired of living with you
You're not a friend
or something I
need or own
and want
to keep
You're something constant
like some nightmare
a story without

a way out to
ever end
But you never really care
How much of my time
and of my life that
You just take
I plan when I can
But with you
things not only bend
You shatter everything
But I power through
What would I do without You
You've become
this thing
a monster I hate
But what would I do without You

Safety Nets

I walked past security
without screaming
but I clutched my blanket
in between my yellow, teethe
as I reached
down
to scratch
the mood ring sea green skin
left from when I fell
against my shin
The stairs are spinning up
when we should
all be
winding down
locked down
but never shut down
only sometimes shut in
like my words
drumming
beats
down over my eyelids
behind them
right under my head
down my chiseled chin
half alive
half past dead

where my hairline meets bone
drumming again
and again
backed up by a sex deprived
strung out saxophone
The brown hair
brown eyed princess
hunkers down
with her arms wrapped
around her knees
huddling above a crimson rose
the rose is red all over
she is red but brown all over
like my words building up walls
all over
with bridges
emotional seas
You know how women are
Time tries to give us thick skin
like my words flowing
out to you
from somewhere sunken deep down in
And Patience
is a virtue wearing thin

Grasping at Love

Cracked dry crimson
My hands
Their skin
Left-side tremors
in closed fisted form
Try forcing it opened
again and again
But yours feel warm
facing palm to palm
gently holding mine
small trembling thin
as if it had been pried
Tracing your lifeline
Your touches begin
to help me feel calm
as fingers intertwine
Nerves and skin
Unsoiled untied

My F Word: Fibromyalgia

Lightning
strikes
hit
my electric
fenced in nerves
My back is a full ice tray
left in a freezer forgotten
Plasma nebula spheres
Burning through finger tips
Eyes swelling with tears
I am needing to be held
Fires push their flames
pressing into my palms
Overpowering Tremors
invade both my hands
My body
is Agony

Your touch calms
me now I breathe
And I settle down
in your heart beat
My body
Is Agony
One part pushes
as all others pull
And It seems so cruel
dealing with the pain
as I am feeling joyful
You will even kiss me
if standing in the rain
I wonder what you can see
Because You still call me
Beautiful

A Poet Without Hands

Hers never clap in rhythm
and never firm are they
or steady for a wave
either for Goodbye
or for hello to say
One tries to sign
gesturing to stay
They never both
can fold to pray
But they both instead
would rather misbehave
They're getting worse and
worse from a tremor's
pain
each day
She needs them
both so very much
for writing her works
of poetry to be her art
as if not given the choice
Playing around with words
became sound for her voice
But now these small hands
their dainty fingers
every part cries in pain
if a pen they grasp to touch
She had to switch from
Sign Language class to
Spanish at PSU

Oh, the power taken
when so many things crippled
hands won't let a person do

But on a mission still are they
help her explain
How she feels
invisible in
society

How nobody really understands
Her messages written in poetry
The girl, the woman, the poet
Despite her insides fighting
her body as if all denying
ever her body notifying
them with an eviction

She will always keep on writing
even with her own two
tremor pain stricken hands
Heating up a beautiful friction
Something only a few friends see
Never is she conceited or full of herself
Unless possibly if full of conviction

Organized Chaos

It seems like these days
everyone is set
Stuck
Settled down
in their own selfish ways
Blinded, bored, and broken
So hard to touch
when so much
that needs to be
said
is
left unspoken
Walking around half dead
Bleeding busted
burning
Pain is living
used to mean learning
Look over your cold shoulder
to see our country getting
tired and older
from history repeating itself
How many times does
it have to say
Blood
Sweat
Tears
We can easily shed
But what about our skin?
Loud and proud

Invisible
Misunderstood
Marginalized
Bullets flying like birds
like planes do
Wild fires spreading
like lies told
Ignoring the young
Killing off the old
So easily we forget
No one can hear the screaming
from all American drug
addicts dreaming
Everyone is being used or using
We're all losing
left alone or
lost
Can't be broken
and broke
stuck
in our handmade
boxes
It seems like these days
No one out there
really prays
It's just something
someone
says

Does anyone really remember
The truth of their shiny
cross necklaces and
sparkly diamond
wedding rings

Seems like we all want to be
the next new Jesus
But we forget
it's his love
Not just his name
that frees
us—any of us
all of us

The ways
that everyone lies
it shouldn't be a surprise
if we have another bloody September

Is our blood really thicker
than the flood water
to every sad
son
And desperate daughter?
What do we really want
to remember
never to forget:
Our national disasters

or our nation's
debt?
American pride
or Christian love?
Or just even only love?
Everyone who has died…

What are we really made of?

Does anyone really know
how much Americans really owe?

God, please bless America
and all of our churches
Wherever we reside
We really believe
we are worth it

You have never been one
making mistakes
Please

Keep giving us hope in our place
to save some smiles
for the human
race
Marching through many miles
Troubling times of trials
Where is the love

when smoke
fills our air
When a pastor feels too tired to care
with his back up against
his own wall

Too many walls

Feeling forgotten
left alone
Not another stone
Cast not another
brick or stone

Hang up those halos

One day church won't be
behind a closed door
The first will be last
Rich will be poor

God reminds us what remains
and what we can take
home with us

And God is everywhere
Closer than it feels
but He's here

In times such as these
Dragged down now on our knees
Praying for a time
When we all
have had
Open
heart surgery
It's a common Christian disease

We let you in our hearts
Lord
Now today
Sorry for the mess
We should have known
when you were coming over
since you have always been around

We need you to make
our home clean
again new
again
so it seems like today
We are all under
construction
But as long as our hearts are open
when the heavy church doors
close
behind
We can see
with faith we're not blind

Existence Is Futile

I wish to be
poetry today
I want to be
the poem
I have writ-
ten already
countless times
so many times
In every way
Yesterday
Years and
years before
Being a human
Or written down
I am still
the thing
Others want
to ignore
Or I get in
their way
No matter what I
am and all I do

No matter
what I say
I'm tired of age
Society's cage
All my
Disabled rage
I'm tired of pain
Of the sun
and I am
actually tired of
all this
persistent
Portland rain
You said you
were tired
even of this
rhyme
Now I'm tired
of you and
how you
keep on staring
at me here

PS To My Existence

Would I be as easy to ignore
If you could see I wasn't
human anymore
A dragonfly can die
A rock might
be crushed
Destroyed
Somehow
But a poem
For me, myself, then
of course I
To be
The poetry
we write
Could stay
around in a way
to be forever enjoyed
Somehow society should see
They could try destroying
the pages by fire
They could torture my humanity
with all its flesh and bone
But the poetry itself
survives on soul food alone

My Old Friend

The way
rain falls
My head pounds
Never not noises
Sometimes spinning sounds
various voluminous voices
Watching wailing walls
But I am not insane
The way I hear rhythmic rain
Pulls poetry pushing pain
I cannot carry a cane
But my skin crawls
Downs my energy
Ghost arms grab my legs
all of it drains
But my
broken
heart
begs
Soothe her suffering soul
Sometimes
storms
stain
I am an empty shell again

You will have to
see through
My blank
brown
eyes
Dressed in darkness
While winter will wait
for summer shadows
A meal
it
swallows
whole
Starvation still sets in
Too little was too late
So Sleep settles
Silent's surprise
This Time paid its toll

Wreckage

Drawing lines in the sand
You wash my dreams
down in a swallow
I hold onto my second helping hand
Arms open wide reaching for a wave
I brush back stray strands of my hair
You stumbled
falling so far away
I saw your silhouette's
strong, tall, hallow
how you stand
and then we
disappear
I had help hanging up my halo
Shadows dancing down
Heaven's horizon
distorted the
plain view
Here we found something is new
But what you didn't know
When you dashed
through this
time
These lines in the sand we drew

Created a cross like design
Out there balancing
the distance between my rhymes
Hovers this embellished
memory that I see
looks like you
Looks the way I wanted us to be

Diagnosed

Jessica Ann
Christian Feminist
Disabled Poet
Shawnee
Woman
Soul
I
Am
Inside
My body
My burden
My captivity
Because when I was born
Scoliosis had sculpted
my curves
They permanently
outline parts
piecing a puzzle of me
I claim it all boldly as mine
But I can't bend,
turn, or twist
And my hips can't move
And I can't shake
But I can love
And I can
break
But I still see
Backbone
Vertebrae
Incision
Spine
Flesh
My way
My mess
I know there's a smile
where You see the frown
From so far
I come
Now
Face
A head
My brain
I frown I
smile

Half empty
Half dead
In denial
A World
Upside
Down
Anxiety
Depression
Fibromyalgia
my nerves erupt
with electricity
Chronic pain
I have to
Feel
Invisible
Chromosome
Syndrome

Missing
parts
am
I

Falling through the Cracks

As your shaking fingers fumble
for your necklace clasp
Solitude screams inside
the shelter
dying to breed
under a breathless gasp
It scurries through
an empty living room
It hums with ceiling fans
Drips with leaking faucets
Flickers in street lamp lights-

Hangs onto thick heavy humid heat
Your eyes adjust but it
Swings against
your anxiety
and eventually
changes
your mood
Crowds clutter around outside
Cursing,
half empty beer cans,
lipstick stained cigarette butts,
chemicals, sewage, waste,
mindless chatter,
the collision of overwhelming
cheap perfume
Oh how
Humanity hungers

for her rights
Stale
Starved
Stagnant
Somewhere
But nothing new
Somebody sideways stares
but just for a minute
then nobody cares again
These days nothing anybody
says seems
true
They won't let you stay alone
for very long
By now it all runs back together
There's nothing else to see
You're never on
your own
In this city
In this generation
You don't really belong
They've reached their limit
Society;
A big box has your life trapped in it

Prayer Poem

I'm winding down a ways
I'm a little lost these days
The Christian claims she prays
But does she call God's name
Does she still cry in her shame
She never feels settled in
Never quite at home here
She tries to be
She tries to feel free
She tries so hard to see God
In everything and
everyone and all
On her knees
Her tears
they all fall
With the leaves
and the rain
She feels so small
inside her pain
God holds onto her there
He loves her there
And She draws near
Even though the Christian
The Child
The Girl
The Woman
The Bitch
The Cow
The Cunt
The Whore
The Lady
The Princess
is so very much afraid
"Here I am," she cries
"I'm tired—so very tired God."
Here He helps her dry her eyes

Drained

Nobody really cares
Nobody really wants to listen
Enough with the ranting rage
Now the zombie sits
in the dark
and stares
with its voice stuck in a cage
A pair of eyes
used to shine
on a pale face without an expression
Angry words
They slip and they spew
And then they all get the best of you
Not to mention
Every time
Part
of the spirit inside dies

Here I Am

I've been walking out in the rain
I try to keep
my head held high
But I'm in too much pain
As strangers pass me by
They don't really see
They don't understand why
I am this way that I just have to be
God I feel alone
though I know deep down I'm not
But when I'm deep in thought
too many voices like to yell
And they like to pretend
Until it's so hard to tell
When I really need
a best friend
if you're really here—here for me
Not just here for everyone
Because God
I've heard it all so many
times before now
But I'm giving the day back to you
But I'm giving my restless nights
I'm giving them all back to you
I'm giving you back the time
After time after time after
time you made for me
I'm still walking out in the rain
But every reflection that it makes

I now see you
And Your light shines on through
I now see you
Every time my heart breaks in two
How ever long the healing takes
I keep walking out in the rain
Even as my heart aches

Even now I see you
And I know you really see me too

Stuffed

The poet sat silently
thoughtful
Words had their way
With her
As if they were
Left unsaid
We could have been
Some stranger's suggestive sigh
But in between the lines we bled
as if ghosts unseen
hallow hearts
half dead
On and on and on again
as you
let us lie below
holding your tongue
to hush echoes of a curse
beaten back under your breath
But we will eventually
be born again
as if made
good or
new
Like these poets we find do

After Hours

Wind-up toys spin around
Steady hands
Your so-called
pretty sparkle life security
perfect job you dream you love

So sick and tired of:
The neighbors
noise—noise—noise—noise
So sick and tired of:

They
Some people
Playing with their big toys
I've fallen in cracks
Underground
Society
We carry the world
on fused backs
Living in our
downcast
heads

Playing pick up sticks
Shooting marbles
match striking light tricks
Late night light tricks
Dream catcher sways some
as if trying to catch one
The moon bounces
down the hall

Still Silence sounds
Little girl ghost
thought it was me She saw
Passing by
Drifting through
Come one, come all
The lucky few
who really
See
Midnight's
Ceiling Show of Shadows
And They say nothing good
happens this late

POETRY STILL EXISTS AND SO DO I 35

Heaven Help Us

How far do you have to reach
before you feel
so suddenly self aware
You want to be honestly real
But not so much today
Settle your restless spirit down
my dearly beloved one
Even though everybody pulls
as hard as they push
at your sweet crooked smiles
forcing you to frown
and it's all
you can express

And it's dreams people shatter
They don't understand
your pain and stress
Wanting to matter
at least seen as civilized
as human

and nothing less
So very sick and tired
of being
So very sick and tired
You feel
this need to explain
Pain changes who you've become
Pain limits what you can be
It's like suffering a loss

We survive the best
we know how to
we know how to
Come back to the cross
Bring tears
Bring all of your loss
Bring your broken heart
You don't need to keep reaching
out into darkness
It's time to rest and then renew

Some Sundays

I wish I never had to pretend
You know how people stared
and those things people said
Figuring out how to be
Everyone's best friend
All put together so well
Always making enough room
Dressed in costume
Nobody there to tell
if that was really me
As soon as we said hello
You turned and you said
Goodbye
By now I should at least know
how to fix some things
and answer Why
But what if I like being broken
Awkward, disabled, sincere,
somewhat soft spoken
And halfway here
Souls still sing while they mend

Family Frustration

Forgetting things
Trying to be thoughtful
didn't recognize her own reflection
had to tell her over and over again
Who she was
Who we became
She kept forgetting her place
saw she was beside herself
as if she stood still
Enough
In front of a full-length mirror
Stuck to the back
of a bathroom door
Nobody there to see
Not anymore
She saw her flesh, her eyes, her soul
that had all buried her underneath
She stood in her reflection
She stood in disbelief
Then hung her towel up again
as if her eyes looked suddenly dry
One tear had left its place
Searching for its expressionless face
And again not a single soul
Was there to see
She had nothing left to do,
To say out loud
Breaking down
under her own weight

Her heart sleeveless and free
She stood as a whole
As someone new
That day
In that moment
She did much more
than slamming that door
Falling apart as her image shattered
With her tears,
She fell to the floor
That day
In this moment
She did so much more
than run away
But she had forgotten
Something very important
We had known at times before
But for some reason
she didn't even try
to stop and pray…

Unmasked

Comparison's moonlight
paled her expression
with porcelain
eggshell
ghost
pigmentation
Something wasn't right
Things felt off
She suffers from an
Unbalanced equilibrium
She keeps an
expression of
being uptight
hanging onto
floating hope
She clings to
laughing lines
drawn up into
codependent
determination
Best of show
for her curves
scoliosis gave
but last place
for her pretty
crooked smile
with one foot
hovering over
a freshly dug

six-foot grave
She feels like
an old frozen
slab of mystery meat
buried in her freezer
She discovers as if
it had stayed fresh
Something she tries to thaw
unlike her tatted on scars
that stay stapled
into her
skin as part of her flesh
This grown woman
stays scared
to death
of ever falling in love again

Off the Record

They stuffed me down in a folder
Filed my heart away under H
for helpless or hopeful
Their decision wasn't unanimous
How should I put pain into words
I wasn't filed directly
next to n for Nobody, or never
or beside p for pain and problems
but how else
should we begin
I'm not that concise
I'm not a gal you meet
when hanging everywhere
I don't feed these selfish blue birds
Not a single solitary one
of them willingly becomes
more than this fragile glass figurine
Always breathless
They never feel
and they never have seen
We've both been set out for display
On our man made, fabricated shelf
My blues keep
their shades drawn
and I shut down
in an overgrown group
I try, but when I dream again
I can't stay asleep every time

And all of us hear
words you scream
So much to say before
you're gone again
And really, nothing here
has been proven
But, I still have to live
with a different new version
of something other than my self

Blunt

Purple Kush and Swisher Sweets
in piles stacked up high
It's all legalized this time
This man child had been
Letting out one long sloshed sigh
Drumming his right-hand fingers
Over and over again and again
He figured
He thought
that he had paid for his crime
He dumped dry ash
into an empty
two eleven beer can
Couldn't believe she'd dumped him
Eyeballing two cats now his pets
He flung an old cigarette case
He had aimed it at them
Shadows crossed his face
He was at home still his place
Left alone to see memory regrets
watching *American Idol* and *Grimm*

Line Dry

Washing your hands
when mine were tied
You washed my brain
cursing out the child inside
You manipulate
But I'm the pain
But I'm a problem to hate
Somebody's stirring spirits
all around everywhere
Now nobody understands
You say let's disappear
Well it sounds insane
You're still scrubbing skin
You tried for so long
You haven't ever felt clean
Our Blood and ink
together they stain
All I could bring to the fight
was my safety pen
Nothing wrong but nothing
if not my words were right

Broken

Weighed down with the world
but my heart hangs empty
Split in two
I should be
Thankful for my angel wings
I try pasting them on
With everything
I feel
But they need a stronger glue
I'm taking my time to heal
But All Memory made by you
stays new and it all stings
I feel with everything
And still I try
not to
But my heart
hangs empty
Weighed down with your world
With my memory you made
The more I try not to see
The more I am afraid
And then I worry that from you
my heart will never be set free

Permitted Fruit

I'll show you my smile
If you show me yours
Awkwardly for awhile
Afterwards
Laughter's
echo blurs
Hang happiness high
on its halo
As eventually we sigh
At least we can try to
feel joy from the soul
Enough to let it show
with our Love Peace
Faithfulness Patience
Gentleness Goodness
Kindness Self Control
All of these we welcome to grow

Twisted

You crossed the
black and blue
punch line
hanging on until I spin

You swing up; high again
Shooting stars through
Somebody else's
Summer sky

Seven years struck
a match to time
These names etched ghosts
out on windows
Your place found
you nearby
But I
Stood still right outside
Invisible
In between a rhyme
where the most
intense pain grows

Love sick, I've been
stricken ill
All around I went missing

Lightning
I let you flash

Scared stiff my heart scars
Why, why, why? But I
But you lie

Nothing was ever
really mine
Calling me stupid again
Calling me fat
Bitch, Cunt, Whore
Boneless paperback spine
Nothing
but an insecure lit-
tle white girl
Okay, I said
another day I'm fine

Thirty-one and
already I feel done

All of this
Love
Leaves me back bone dry

I fell
I went down
You let me down

Remains:

that it would be my dream
that I would
like it that way
You could do better
And I should want more

Thirty-one

But I've long since before
I ever could feel
As if I were
Real

Thirty-one, and
what shows?

These memories
Strike, and the blows
With sticks and
stones, they blur

Sewn Back Together

Fires rise up so far
soon they have built their wall
Still some tears fall
Over my own
Walls I built through
Years of shame
Of guilt
And it's like nothing I try alone
ever dries them all
But with you
You take back everything I feel
No matter how dark
My nightmares
became
You reclaim all I ever have felt
Then you change
my name
You guard as you guide
And You don't hide your face
I never have to search
for long
Far and wide
For a sign of your grace
Every day miracles
surround us all
Even in the midst of our shame
Digging down deeper still
You take back
our guilt

The bad the cruel
the mean
Everything ugly we have seen
It's not what your will
has ever meant
Lead us through our sacrament
We need you for souls
only you help
mend
Lead us through our sacrament
Here you become
not only God
Here you dry our eyes
Here we can call you friend
Here the fire calms and it dies
Here you help the nightmares end

Saved

He said, she said, he did
And I hid my soul from him
Eventually from—everyone
Now try to mark me down as
Other than female
Other than human
Any—other—thing
—Something—he can't see

If only my insides were just as pale
like the flesh
I have been given to wear
This skin—that—I—am in
I am in here
I know or
I thought so
But you don't see
what he called me
and it's all in my head—he has been
Nobody could understand
—not really

But I am still a Native here
As much as they will try
to deny I am Shawnee
Every other day
He had to say
Stupid
Little

White
Girl
He cut his way in
He called me Bitch
When I was a woman

I am as real as my pain
He'd break me again and again
He laced everything good
As if he was medicine
His words cut again and again
Blood usually leaves a stain
But not the blood I'm washed in

Or Something Like It

I was left
thoughtless
with half a mind
an empty chair sits by
trying to not think at all
A migraine
was once
bittersweet
Let the world come
visit me
just as long
as long as well enough
is left alone
my rustic thoughts
are confined
to the heart
of my soul
which I had
for breakfast
one day
The other night though
I caught myself
in a dreamless sleep
But a nightmare slipped
through an opened window
When will reality
separate
me
from
the world
They all walk on eggshells
tiptoeing around me
But what is the use
If we really
are just passing time
I have come to fear
the most in the least
I suppose
I know
with one thought
I was left
to write
At least a blind man
could see me
for who I really am
What a widow
would seem to know
and all of our own
perfume jars
lost in a crowd
trying to travel like the stars
Who wants to see
the giant man
behind his cloud
Breathless wondering
how important I
think You are
with whatever it is

the humans all do
How
can we not
feel everything
the world spins around
not the lost and found
But
I
was trapped in that
one box labeled
Miscellaneous

God Bless America

Yes we have the homeless,
the hungry and poor
people
We think we could eat
a horse when we think
we're so hungry
we must be starving
for more than attention
We think we will never
eat again when we
feel so full and stuffed
When are we thoughtful
When are we fed up
When is it enough
for us to stop
wanting
more
of this and that
God bless us
Americans
given the freedom
to feel fat and
to feel poor
Pray for us Americans
When we can't see
what others
endure

Wait Here

Hearts beat
underneath skin
Been having
what I call
an ugly day
but I didn't
look at it all
in this way
But I am tired
of hiding behind
this imag-
ery of me
this ugly pic-
ture I saw
from my
insecurity
Took a TV show
for me to find
what others
would say
they see
The picture
might look ugly
But the girl
is pretty
Hearts beat
underneath
I'm not on TV
or a model
in some
magazine
People today
in the world
define
beauty easily seen
But their
definition
It isn't mine
Look at
me
Not at my
breasts
Not at my butt
Not my face
So what
you see are
the body parts
of beauty
kept hidden
You can laugh at
a photograph
but the girl
you see her face
captured in
place
But do
You see
An ugly picture
taken of a
pretty girl
and of a beau-
tiful woman-
Hearts beat
underneath skin
Mine beats over
and over again

We the People

Love Hate Love Hate
Love Hate Love
Hate we put up
for debate
God saw Satan
Suddenly smile
Since he's been set free
We let the devil
reincarnate
bargain for his vic-
tory to control
Sanity's staircase spirals
down until shadows
all but disappear
Will God see
more than one soul
searching for home
What reason is
enough to spare
Stranded I'm
out of reach

Underground I am
waiting in the
middle being
so self aware
Frozen
Fading
Fainting wallflower
All this soft light
left to devour
What can a lit-
tle mouse
do to guide humanity
Poets like me push
out political poetry
Voices of power
Problem is how I
like to hide when
I know I should
stand up and read

Dear America

In God we trust to shed His Grace
on thee, on us, on you, on me
and on our mother land
as we stand strong
and still free
She's
Holding
her ground
with your voice
Heavy hearts pound
with breathless choice
Blood Crimson Native soil
becomes buried by blind bodies
as they look mostly black and white
We believe there to be just
simply those wrong
or those right
of us left here now to fight
And as Americans
we want to
win
But the Natives want to belong again

Naturally

Eyes squinting in
the summer sun
Knees bent in a dog park
She casts her head
down to look
Searches
for four leaf clovers
She searches until
she finds one
Children from a day care
playing with laughter
off to the side
make her
smile
Innocent emotions
They have them
but hide none
as dogs when they bark
never appear shy
The woman
watched the
moment pass by
She felt insecure
She felt too self aware
searching all the
clover fields
She tried so hard not to care
what people had to be
thinking of her
But this time, she made sure
anxieties and worries
would subside
so she could have some fun

From My Heart

In between these lines
of all
poetry
and time
Of laughter
or possibility
Life writes
our story
about
Us
As I pray
you will have
even sweeter dreams
and better good
Mornings
Common expressions
our love refines
into these rare jewels
like the treasure
You've become to me
So soon things we do
with all things we say
really mean I love you

Looking Up

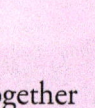

Melting hearts run together
Egg yolk folds in the center
Brewed us a pot of storms
Warm and Strong
Double—shot
Dark and Rich
press in use wrist
whisk troubles away
Waiting became past tense
I'm thinking out loud
Talking to myself
Watching my weight
Neck hairs rise fast
A sudden chill
rushes through
goosebumps dec-
orate my arms

Feeling stared at
from behind aways
But I am alone
content and okay
with my irrelevant rambles
too self-aware
trying to be grown
sitting with a drink
for once not diet soda
my soul swims in
trying to look alive
Just said I was "fine"
like burned oven
baked bacon
Nobody complains
Hopeful here
for happiness

Little Things

it can
be like
Tuesday
taped on
chocolate
love notes
a sandwich
hands made
we do we say
as thoughts of
love remain real
until so much time
has passed and gone
but together we still stay
because we weren't afraid
of expressing the way we feel

During the Day

Sidewalks set in sticky gum
She set scattered leaves on
And I was set to making fun
of these things all about her
These things that seem
random as if in a dream
Small talk trades
Conversation
for some
memory
as most of mine fades
Tomorrow can't be
like right now as we
can't stay just how we
moments earlier
I see now we were
And I know
Nothing is really so random
Like being here then gone
God gives it all meaning
and everything reason
In life he takes us far
As far as we can go
It's not so much in asking
My sin and I to welcome
He won't make fun
We can cry
as I do
and so very often

In a whisper
In a sigh
He calls us by and by
To Come
Dear child come
Come child just as you are

Make Believe

Stuffed animals sit for tea
They wait expressionless
with empty beaded eyes
but they're watching me
They can't guess or see
my very clever disguise
But it's never what I'm
really supposed to be
But I'm never too old
to pretend or to play
Their stuffing wears
out over the years
while mine sheds
blood and tears
We were made
very differently
They never do
say how they
feel as I do
when I am
afraid of
being
real

Mismatched

Down here watching all the clothes spin
Saw a sad soppy sock missing its twin
Lint, pennies, string, wet stick of gum
A blue button, wadded paper, a pen
Emptied and pulled out pockets
Can hear the swishing some
Laundry looks like poetry
Without words to fill in
But can anybody ever understand
all of these things we mean?
No matter how honestly
hard the humans try
We won't ever all wash out totally clean

Off Trail

In the summer
sun's shadows
walking around
some place
you're just a
lonely man

Empty eyes look
halfway down
and find you
swimming
with only
a frown on all
the way
Syllables slip some
subtle swigs; they
run by lines with
whistled wind
but loosen
your grip
Soon, your reality's all shattered
as it liquifies
your thoughts
stirred up by
the storm
You now see coming
fast like giants
stomping across your
dreams
they rock back

and forth as
you swish
your memories all
over all around
And you wish
you could
be blind
And you hope
there's no
more
still a float drifting behind
When did you
swallow
your deflated pride
just enough so
you're warm
just enough so
you know
letting go now of all
you thought ever
had mattered
Old man, you
look so very old
Are you so sure
you know
now where
you're goin?
which road you want
to take your last?

breathe away
Old man
so sad
so senselessly
so scattered
You sigh and
drop your
dad's glass marble
shooter it leaves
your brown
wrinkled thumb
and your brown
pruned
finger
tip
You let it roll on with
the mud caked hill
Can't take your
eyes from it
no you can't remove
your eyes off
from it still

Here

Finally

something

you have to face

Prism Reflections

Adjusting to the light
I see now in front of
you but no more
in front of
me since becoming
as plain
as this view we see
all of them they are
behind a non
smoking screen
She was here but
eventually has gone
through it all
tonight
What's it all
Mean
Scrape my shadow
from the ceiling
to the floor
Spit and
shine
Get back in line
But I'm afraid
of the dark
and to be
all alone
As if it all were mine
Something I could
be sold and own

The possibility
If I was right
left in my poetry
adjusting to the light

As I wish I might
sooner see
You are
My
ocean sun set view
You become
Poetry
My
Poetry
becomes You

Sincerely

With so many ways to love
How do we know the right one
How do we know what to dream of
Put your best face forward
and then up at a
faceless
Sun
But we've been
down here
before
blind
deaf
loud
We have so many souls to possess
A thousand eyes
With harder tries
How many times
did you have me did you take me
did you tell me did you make me
With your hands
or your heart
Your souls
Did love
help us undress
Honestly when do we bear it all
Tumbling blocks crumble
like Clay as anxiety
mocks so soon
Society talks

back in a
sermon
But I've heard enough of them
I don't need to learn today
I want my words of us
to do more than say
how to burn
to water
mother
Earth
Pillars of salt
Nothing is your fault
You're doing everything right
It's just that you're not really okay
Step into the light from
this shadow
of mine

Alone with God

Silver lines the sky today
The golden eye hides its face away
And I sit with my mug of tea
A lazy cat stretches nearby me
And I know even though I can't see
The words my heart hears
through the years
all you say
In my tears I have to sigh
Though my hands tremble
in pain
I still find comfort
Your love comes down in the rain
My God understands
How things have
come to be
Where his beauty leaves his trace
When I need to hide my face
When I need to cry alone
My God watches
Over me
His love rains down from his sky
For all of us to see
What he has known for so long
Even now
I still stay strong
Even if I am feeling weak today
My heart can still pray
even though I don't speak

I worship you with my poetry
as others dance
while some people sing
I don't have to move for you
to see my praise
The lines dance for me
When I can't clap physically
Each word claps loud like thunder
You feel love
from every phrase
When I want to bend on my knee
when I want to pray that way
You somehow still see
what all I mean
What I wish I could do physically
Just as Jesus spoke
His words broke through the storm
You give power to my poetry
Your love written down
You hold onto me
As I write, you're keeping me warm

Come Closer

Hello do you see
me down here
Sometimes like
right now
I need this world
to roll itself away
Like the stone
from the tomb
rolled
open
as Jesus rose
but then stood
at first unknown
Invisible to
human eyes
God in the flesh
as the son
Mary
at
first couldn't
recognize
her child that day
She couldn't
keep you
on her
own
or make you stay
for her alone
Like this
world
we share you
God and son
But some-
times we feel
unrecognized
disbelieved
and even
alone
We think
maybe
You've lost
your power
when we pray
for you to
help us
heal
despite that
final hour
all it took
all you gave
We couldn't look
at Jesus on the cross
or believe when
we could
see
the stone
from an empty tomb
You rolled away
as if tears He
cried in His
sweat as if
He didn't ever bleed
Only You can
send Him
for us
again
As I wait here
Sometimes I need
this life to pass away
It's so hard
lately to pray
All I know is I'll see
you sometime
soon
but You never
said when
Please while we
are waiting
tears roll
down
from
my pain only
you can see
But do you really
recognize me

Autopilot

Electrical currents
course through
violet veins
A nebula
fire ball
people
never
see
turns
twisting
like they all do
underneath the skin
searching a million souls
Not all so forgotten
We aren't all
drones
yet
Day to day
life
drains
our vessels
While storms brew
Nothing new
refills
a human brain
Problems
People
Pain
this world
welcomes to

Facing the World

Always the ques-
tion How are You
We lie that we're fine But I am
not going to Tell the truth in
your reply Here's mine
My body feels like
Hot
Fires
Flame
Nebula
Elephant
Car Wrecks
Bowling Balls
Lightning Storm
Pens and Needles
consume spread run
me down run me over and
shoot through veins and tissue
But you can't see how I feel
the way they force me to
like hot flashes when
night sweats and
cold chills like
feverish flu
But I don't feel sick
the same way most people do
You know about Fibro
when it flares
And I can tell if someone cares
The way to stay inside to
be stuck at home
More than one
thing wrong
And More
are right
You see
but not
like I
do
at least Most of the time
But I say it's still okay
and so are you

The Homeless

Cold winds stir this melting pot
around Until we see their faces
Until we give them our thought
Until instant recognition traces
all places their raw hearts had
sought as they fought Hunger
of a desperation we know not
So be thankful for rest tonight
in a clean and safe warm bed
For all that food you were fed
And for that shelter overhead
Their faces I find everywhere
Out of mind and Out of sight
Still they are all in plain view
But it is more difficult to see
so up closely in front of you

Liberty

Flowing with milk and honey
Men welcome
We call all evil
These women
See
who
calls illegal aliens
foreign
It is us
versus
them these days
We welcome you
so called Americans
Interbred conformity
Processed we've been fed
The Lady turning her back
frozen in this place
Heart of stone
She's cold
Alone
As Time stands still for her
She welcomes the poor
the hungry and tired
Immigrants most
of us we were
Baby crying
Mammas pat the tiny head
Dying to get in and
be called American

Crammed
Jammed
Packed
in tight
so full like sardines
Life left
homes
streets
paving
it all in
golden
dipped
dreams

If You lady could stand to see
So these days your silence
from New York across
to California your
silence loudly
at all of us
screams

Under Construction

City Skyscrapers far
and wide to see
have me
feeling
small
Remembering
who marched around
that wall in Jericho
If I had lived
in Bible land
Feet thun-
dered sound
like trumpets blown
As God's hand
in it all was
shown
Later in our history
stone thrown
as people said call
us
Christian
Even later on
stood a great wall
again in it Berlin rose
Orders
for
borders to close
Eventually
torn

Anxieties
Agony
Fears
Pain
build
walls
inside
bodies
we hide
throughout the years
they've grown so
tall and wide
still grows
Curtain drawn up
with windows
The ghost
I hide behind
Feeling Trapped
strapped in
there
with darkness
We reside
As I do
begs the
big question
Why should you
want to fur-
ther divide
the human race

For
Room
to breathe
You need your space
You're so well
known
But
You
too
will
fall
Wall
By
Wall
Come
crumb
bling
down
brick by brick by
glass by glass
and by stone
Heart by
head
As We stand on solid
American ground
not so small
are we
when by God
we're led

Back Spasms

Two
Fisted
punches
hit
from
under
her skin
Two Rods
Tough steel
Yes
She nods
Enough to feel

Turning Over Leaves

History spun backwards
now stares at me
I reside here
to hide to dwell
It's not so hard to tell
what the world's looking like
I observe her from inside my shell
As things are then as they were
I know I have a hard enough
time trying to feel well
It's highly likely as
true for you
My eyes
peering out from my safety net
So much needs God's touch
But by now there shouldn't
be any reasons why you
two haven't both met
This world of ours all of us share
is looking less like our home
Looking less like we care
We have her looking
more like hell in a
living nightmare we can't forget
Some days I venture a ways
I reluctantly go out there
for a time in society
It's harder there
to tell the differences

in between other
souls and me
All of us try
Having
fun
But it's so difficult a lot of work
Everyone trying to feel happy
Everyone tries feeling free
when it's hard enough
for us trying to be
something the world wants to see

Lost Innocence

Let's stop acting like we're so grown
Let's disappear
and stay alone
At home today
Now you see me now others don't
Childhood games
we safely play here
And Let's make believe
that We can become anything
and end up being anywhere
with fancy fake names
of important royalty
Yes You can be
a noble king
I'll be your kind queen
Time for tea
from a half empty cup
You claim it's full
until the mean
monsters
are woken up
Our castle's cast
under a witch's spell
And she took
my ring
We now have to kiss
like love is true
as if in it we
fell like

wishes do in a secret wishing well
Let's pretend our
childhood is
calling us
to play
Nobody to tell us no
or say we're wrong if
we don't follow their rules
they persist we
will obey
that We have to look
Or dress
in a certain way
as if they
get along better
than we do
having
fun in our dream world together
without this society
labeling what
all we do
and analyzing what all we say

Native Territory

Run fingers through
your liquid gold
Baby
been
fed milk for free
since small enough
for mamma to hold
But's craving a new
nutritious necessity
Heaven has paved
its streets with
more than
sweets
This promised land
We've all been told
flows with pure milk
and thick rich honey
But no sinner
God there
Greets
But you're
just a fresh beginner
There Might be room
God forgives
as a baby
lives
as one whole
with a heart and soul
But it's you they see
fingering your black
loosely drained tea
They do understand
A white man's
greed
These days they do
know Unfortunately

Lifelike

Through her ebony eyes
Down to her
soul's scars
Blues sing solemn sighs

She sees fireflies

Her childhood captured
dreams shut up tight
in Mason jars
More than words she
wants to write
Behind her masking names
She likes to hide
She hides alone

She prays in a whisper
Pleading for peace
Still

Unknown

A
Trembling left hand
Folds as it tightens
in agony
against her—side

As if you could understand
Nothing ever feels right

From her faults, her flaws
her restless spirit seeks release

Solitude signs
its signature with a certainty
an audience would
never hear or see

Speechless Words

Our minds hang on them
like a thousand ribbons
discarding all pink or blue
so we stay stronger
than their sticks and stones
which we have stolen
made our own
to last longer
Moments like these have thrown
caution to whirlwinds
We storm about like
the monsters
we have become
No more hiding under
our childhood beds
We wax and wane
hanging our haloes
high above the clouds
Our gift of life is the present
but we love talking
about our past
as long as the stereo-
type should last
Then we rest our weary heads
against our moth-
ers' broken backs
but we were careful
of what to wish for
as we stepped on sidewalk cracks
Even the odds were against us
with our hands tied
now measuring our
sticks and stones
by memory
until somehow justified
If time heals all wounds
then why are you standing still
turned into a pillar of salt
since you were caught
looking over your shoulder
Our biggest regret is free will
as we keep getting older
We love in spite of ourselves
and nothing is ever my fault
But why do I keep talking
to myself
I know
Yes
I do see you
I see all of us
I know where my heart is
so I am never alone
even when no one else is home

24/7

Where has the
day gone
Where has
time flown
Are you having
any fun
acting grown
staying up
past dawn
Or are you
busy at work
Always on the run
Lost your place
where the
line
had once been
drawn
to balance pros
and cons
or did you forget
how to play
Maybe you
lost the bet
Maybe you're not
even up
yet
Maybe you just
are having
One
Beer
a Soda or
last Cigarette
Dying to sur-
vive here
Not as easy to
surprise
You
have
nothing
Nothing at
all to fear
Anything you
wish you
had
already known
They say live
for today
and it's easier
alone
You want to believe
that it can still
get worse
Dreams, goals,
and plans
you try to
think you
can achieve
Practice
then rehearse
But you're just
so naive—
Really nobody
really
ever understands
why you wear
your heart
out on a rolled
up sleeve
Or why you
carry so
much on your
shoulders
and in your purse
Why You can't
escape yourself

Even if you've
checked out

—you still
can't leave

Emblem

Through my eyes walk in my shoes
Reality realizes perspectives
choose all the Don'ts
and all the Do's
For
freedom
comes dressed
up in blush ivory black out
blood skin tears shed striped blues

Empty Pockets

No sleep tonight as you turn left
and then tossing right
from side to
side we try as we do
to hide
undercover
and We hold on tight
to these day dreams We've had
forever awhile long, long time
Can candidates care less
if they commit
crime
What's their greatest defense
What wall will we climb
Compete confess
We want change
to make sense
You've given us your two
Well now we want it worth a dime

Forgotten Memories

God found light in the dark
And I found poetry
in a ginkgo tree
staring back at me was art
You held the jar
with fireflies
inside
we watched
as they
would glow then die
made rings from their guts
stuck on our fin-
gers like gum
Night adventures together
We found shining bits
of broken jewelry
and metal pieces
from construction
rings in the church
parking lot

Things others had lost
Memories
my childhood saved for me
We stumbled on treasures
like these
Four leaf clovers I
always found
in grassy patches
at rest stops
Off hiking trails
Along cracked sidewalks
cigarette butts scat-
tered all around
Trash and hidden treasure
But I found poetry
has been born again
in everything everywhere
God already has
said it was good

(Written 9/11/2001, right as the second tower was being hit;
I was in the library at school and just needed to write right away
as if something guided me then and there.)

Twins

Crash into freedom
Branded with scars
Swinging on rusted hinges
Hang the stripes and stars
Heartbeats race
To the chaotic flow
While a broken face
Still waits below
Who are we in fear?
What were they here?
Press against the walls
As Freedom's Eye falls
Innocence crumbles
With the sight
Capture your truth
Hold on tight
Build up the bravery

To a beating heart
Once lost in slavery
Now lost in the dark
Who are we now?
What has pain done?
Please show us how
We can stand as one
Reach out the hands
Through the towering billows
Of hatred and spite
If Truth understands
What the bought
freedom knows
Have we learned
but to fight?

To Be Overcome

Sometimes I have to laugh at pain
even when it makes me
cry sometimes I cry
for joy but hardly
ever is it fun
to feel so
much
real sadness
as it all exists in this
beautifully
chaotic
world where we let the devil reign
Sometimes I have to scream
if I make any noise out
loud at all without
human restrain
if even just in
protest to
shout
great opinions of shear disdain
When will it all bring us all
down on our knees
as in a gesture
to pray to
pray it
all
away—to pray the devil away
Are we so much in
danger of

hate
where love will not ever prevail
Is it really right now
too late
Have
Too
many souls gone so far astray
when have we had enough
of our self-afflicted pain
for it to say and to
admit all of us
together fail
but remain
humbly
at your feet Dear Lord
Oh Dear Mighty Reverend God
Here now we come here
now we come just
as we are so
remarkably broken and maimed
Dare we say a single word
however muttered out
in prayer as you
hold out
your
opened arms
as it is so declared
by your Grace we're reclaimed

Grief Stricken

Usually, in autumn, leaves fall
With Winter, the Snow
And Spring rain
Usually after
sun shines
on pain
on sorrow
Usually there's light for us all
But for this Summer
action and then
duty did call
officers of
the law
As these dark times
protest against
racial crimes
God, we
pray
help broken hearts
melt as we raise
them up to the
Summer sun
so they might begin to thaw

Social Insecurity

Slapping on another street
Asphalt
Concrete
Built roads
Saturated soil
A full month of rain unloads
Below pairs of dried up feet
Souls travel through society
I look up from underground
But the people
Strangers
I see
never do look at all like me
Roads repaired from rain
Cities were man-made
But I am under
construction
As people
try to fix
all of
me
But I am working on my pain
Afraid people won't like
what they would see
What I won't ever be
When it's too much work
Being placed in their society
I fell in between
I am stuck in a crack
as an invisible ghost unseen

My Favorite Season

Falling
autumn
leaves
laughter
all around
us
then
underneath
my memories
nestle
Old ones
continue
to
open
blessings
everyone
remembers

The Pursuit Of...

Notice the rhyme there
Take your time
A good rhyme scheme
makes everything better
Better
Letter
Feather
Weather
Notice the "thers"
the "tts"
Well done

Overdone
overtime
Timeless
turned over
like Shakespeare rolling over
in his grave
to let everyone see
his good side now
Like a pig in a blanket
not the kind you can eat
A lamb led to the slaughter
was never a little lost lamb

A nice comfy
woolen sweater
Your Aunt Teresa knitted
Mary had one
Worn inside out
You know, the nursery rhyme
Not the virgin Mary
The other one
A classic
Oh, you're not from here
then you might
not have heard

We are all God's sheep
Like a herd of deaf
dumb sheep
God's little children
but life
gets to be a bitch
where the sidewalk ends
A never-ending story
lives happily
ever after
Almost always never

POETRY STILL EXISTS AND SO DO I

No One Knows

Where night-
mares are born
Never returns
Not again
A formless soul
See your shadow
by a candle
light burns
Which are you?
Burnt out
faceless
or lit
Wondering
in the sands
untouched
reaching
up hands
Always
has been
here long before
you
split
Dry dust
down you bit
A hard fall
to catch

Taste grains
salty sand
sea salt
washed up
on dry land

Wake up!

Sweaty
Shaken
not stirred
like
the clammy
fish hand

Suddenly

The earth stops
spinning
A chill hangs
our air
up to dry
so
tightly
wound

Bring him back!

My
hands are tied
Let my alarm
unwind

Sliding into
dreams
Running around
in a brace
Her ghost keeps
grabbing
your ankles
from below
nowhere to run
no one to follow

Only reality
the few
the grotesque
heartbeat

Be still
Calm
down
Try to relax

Deep breath in
And hold
Shhhhhhhhhh.

Hesitation

Wait for it
Patience waits
for you

Missing out on
missing
someone
A lost love

Done doing

Balance
B
r e
a
k it
down

A fear of clowns
or spiders

A fear of
humans
of going out
Self Loathing
Anxieties

Tell me your
deepest dark-
est secret:
Happiness

Holding on
to dear life
Dear Life,
How are we
today?
Barely hang-
ing on
Drowning
In mainstream's
midstream
Confessions
A confinement
A confident
confidant
A daydream

Writer's block
writing blank
reality
checks for:
What we do
What we want
Dream of
Wish for
Worry about
Losing control
when
Never comes
true

Multiple
personalities
The living dead

Out of Touch

Doing nothing much
Just sit there
Lie down
Push the tears back
into your skull
to get it in
your thick head
The dream
comes and goes
Lie down
in the darkness
A quiet whisper
of shadows
No one quite knows
they bring
a well-known comfort
to you
with the voices
from mistakes
Choices
you wish you could make
now instead

But no
Know
we were never good
just as it was
Never just fine
when you were mine
So my dear
How are you today?
Bless your little heart
Crushed and torn apart
What is that you say
Just look in the mirror
Right back at me
Senseless to touch
Doing nothing much
Nothing less
Just how we felt
Oh, I'm sorry
to bother you
I was just talking
to myself

Expression

Sharp shooting stars
We scurry to my soul
We reach a scorpion
scratching my throat
We break down wall
after wall on our way
searching for a heart
buried six feet under
anxiety's depression
Melancholy's agony
it holds the grudges
I carry in the shame
memory missed
sculpts some scars
patches eye covers
over a hellish portal
I find up in my mind
where I allow a wild
imagination roam to
feel a little bit
like home
Laughing in a smile
we watch the child
make ink smudges
look like a mud pie
But she took a bite
from a red apple of
my black light eyes
rolling two back up
You ride their stars
back into my heart
We fall and we rise
from the soil swept
clean from my feet
Your magic fingers
press light tracing
touches help heal
Feeling butterflies
in a breath drawn
out of my control
You find my soul
You settled into me
with arms wrapped
all around the night

Dear God

When tears are my
words, I pray
You listen to me cry
Still you stay
Oh God
I need you nearby

When sorrow is
all I can show
from feeling so
much pain
You let me know
it's okay
If I'm not all okay,
I can complain
And it won't
make you go
When others leave
I still believe
You stay by and
let me grieve

When shadows
hide my face
in these times
I seem so small
All I see, it seems
Is my broken heart
my shattered dreams

All my spirit
knows is grace

Oh God, oh my Lord
Still in this dark-
ened place
I see you waiting
around for me

You still stay
One day at a
time, you know
When I will praise
without tears
without a broken
heart of sorrow

For now, I might
just cry
and want to complain
as if you didn't know
my reasons of why

But still you stay
as you remain

Listen as I whis-
per in this cry

Amen

Welcome

We like to slam
doors around here
A yelling match
or
The crying game...
What noises we
make tell us apart

Which favorite
depression glass
bowl or favor-
ite mug got
broken this week?

And I'm just
another female poet
writing out her
emotions....

Sweep the barefoot
pricking pieces
under the cat
vomit-disguised
earthy rustic
brown rug
and I'll pretend
not to hear
all the muttering
curses under
His lovely
coffee
Turmeric

sunflower
seeds
red
wine breath
But at least your
Bible's not caked
with dust
buried beside the
family dictionary
hiding forgot-
ten pressed four-
leaf clovers
found by your
oldest daughter
or leaning up
against the
Self Help/
Theology section
or the collection of
overdue library books
we mean to read but
prefer binge-watching
some doctor dramas
Their problems
stay on Netflix
listening all about
the latest
local news
and where the
mass shootings
have happened
this time
don't forget the

counted
totals
of
Covid deaths
listed by state
then by county

At least we wear
the right masks
and we've got-
ten vaccinated
and we wash
our hands
Secretly wishing
some people
will always have to
stay socially distanced

What would it
be like now
if He was still here?

And I'm just
another poet
writing out feelings
as if family and
friends listen
as if people really care

But really: Hi.

How are You?

Iniquities

So called beauty sleep

Did you wash
your hands
long enough
to sterilize
Then draw
up a plan
for at least
an hour or two
Make certain
the soap
stays
out of your eyes
Now
Are you
nice and clean
Since the big
bad world
has been
so
cruel and mean?
Did you wash
the pain down
a drain?
though
it is not fear
that will stain
Keep from the mess

as tension
brews up stress
It will all
come back to you
not to mention
It will all
come pouring down
over you
So you best
get some good sleep
the kind
with an empty mind
but a heart
full of dreams
safe beside darkness
where your eyes
won't see
to keep
in a deeper rest
No use
with counting
on sheep

Don't you worry
Nothing
can break in
You just are broken
in two
As the rain

is all coming down
outside
You can hold
the covers closer
over your weary head
but fall asleep
to the peaceful sound
because
nothing touches you
like the bad things we do
or have to say
You're still just fine
Tomorrow
is another day
for sorrow
Nothing gets to you
as long as
you act

nice
and look clean
but nothing
touches
you
but what
gets rid of sin
So sweet dreams
and goodnight
The monster
hides under the bed
Tomorrow
the big bad world
is waiting for you
And that pain
and the fear
you are sleeping with
will be brand-new

Scattered Brain

Wash tension
down a drain
Roll my pain all away
The Mysterious
Unknown
They
Let them roll off
of your back
Our World
Thunder
Stone
roll
if you say so
I'm rolling
my eyes
at pain
today
They
say pray
Tonight
as I do
I ask
let all my love stay
just roll my pain
so far away
Anxieties
attack
me
So many tears roll
across my face
salty to taste
I'm feeling
small so
I need Your grace
God don't leave
Don't let me
go to that
place
without at least
a tiny mustard
seed of Faith
I roll over on
to my other
softer
side
I have never
found rest
To feel a
peace
The kind
You have
to provide

Internal Dialogue

Too much time
Up in my head
Afraid to sleep
My mind stays
Alert and busy
Train after train
I hear engines
of my thinking
My mind plays
games with me
World of words
Enjoys my pain
Stories chatter
Memory haunts
my mind's attic
rummaging all
through boxes
So much light
it all seems off
Eyes squinting
see fuzzy color
remnants spot

But I am in pain
in my bed alone
with this crowd
Is all inside me
driving through
my dreams and
night terrors of
everything and
of nothing at all
I'm overthinking
talking to myself
as if that's news
or surprises You
I keep on talking
to myself and I
expect helpful
and true replies
Is it safe enough
to close my eyes
as sleep weighs
me down it tries
to pull me under

Momentarily

Laughing has aged
Ruby red wine
While the past waits in line
To see the monster
History has caged
With the wild mangled hair
And deep dark eyes
Stare
They freeze fear into place
Injury takes their grace
To make
The final appearance
On center stage
Pulling out
A splinter
With some rabid rage
What ills remain
Reasoning to last
Taking the rabbit
Out of his hat
Breaking the habit
Of this and that
To forget the past
Never question why
Open to close
Up and down
But I oppose
The smiles who frown
For all to know
I have come so far
by knowing what to hide
and what to show

Lingering in Limbo

I lost sight when the
rain kept falling
thought I'd been fol-
lowing my dream
turned out a gnat
was caught
flew into the cor-
ner of my eye
I heard my voice whisper
when I wanted to scream
Somebody said I can
keep crawling
Keep the pace with
my self-esteem
losing in this human race
But I'm so unique
I am one of a kind
Get off my back
And off my case
Please stop keeping track

I know I've made mistakes
But the fires died sev-
eral years ago
But my walls hide my heart
There's a hole carved inside
So I thought I
could just pack
it all up again
and I'd move
Push problems past pain
Now and then
possibly prove
that I'm not really insane
Barely breathing for now
Someday or somehow,
sometime soon, I'll start
somewhere
somehow
will stop feeling hollow

Well, Well, Well

Back roads
Backbone
Backwards
Understand my tone
Underneath the blood stained skin
Burdens, problems, heavy loads
Smiles seeking soaring spirits
Settling down restless hearts
With God's love living light
Singing somewhere softly
It is well with my saddened sickened soul
piecing back together inner peace
to let go
mankind's cruelty took
advantage of my love
I needed to be missed by someone
Who seemed to care, but then
I soon went missing
As conscious as I became
Then suddenly so very unaware
But I take it all to God in prayer
Bent
Broken
Burdened
Even so. Even so…

Day Drums

While the blind man hums
He lets the little
runaway girl cry
Her dreams have been sold
for daylight
to stop in time
from falling backwards bent
out of shape
like formless empty space
Sunsets melt the sky
like churning butter creams
The blind man
holds his cup
hoping for a sampled taste
if promises should
pretend to keep
and hold him fast asleep
He wins his buttered bread
in his dreams
when everything else
has been tried
when everything else
like crisp fallen leaves
dried him up
He lets the lost run-
away girl cry
Cold Winter rains washed
away her soul
so she sold it to
the devil again
when she found him
sitting down
the road on his side
She swallowed him whole
then stepped back
in her box
Finding out her pillows
were really rocks
like the walls she built
to shelter sickened
fears she felt

Unfiltered

One day, I had
taken my heart
out on one of our strolls
around a park
Barely before sunset
Enough hours before dark
Anyway, I some-
how stumbled
I tripped. Then I
suddenly fell
in a magical wishing well
Looking up from
underground
I saw
some
strange
shadows
of
souls
stomping
silence
back
into
sound
My soiled hands compound
sifting through muddy dirt
drudging up my dreams
I was collecting dust
as an afterthought
But then I forgot
I had buried my
hurt and distrust all around
I don't think I'm alone
But I can't climb
over walls they surround
I'm worried what
will be there
What I will see and hear
I'm so used to being
Invisible, Unheard,
and Unknown

Acceptance

The rocking chair
sits empty.
And so does she;
the woman barely there,
but burdened oh so heavily.

The woman cra-
dles her body.
Her arms wrap
tightly around.
She wears her flesh
as a brace;
keeping more
than her bones
bagged in their place.

But she rocks
back and forth—
trying not to shed
more tears.
And, she feels every-
thing at once.

But, she's search-
ing for her worth.

She sobs silently, now,
as she hunts.
Her head and heart hope
with fears.

The woman now
sits empty;
rocking steadily in her chair.
And, that is all of her
you would see.
But, she wouldn't
blame you,
anymore, for stopping
by to stare.
Because, her spirit
has escaped,
Her heart has broken
Free.

Interference

I'm sorry I'm not the friend
that you need right now.
After my grandma died
my mom got cancer
and then I found out I
was pregnant and it's
been a lot of anxiety and
depression for most of
this year. It's not personal
to you, I'm struggling to
stay connected with
everyone this year.
I'm sorry I didn't text you to explain sooner, it's never my intention
to hurt you or anyone else, I just really suck at communicating and
I'm very sorry that my actions hurt you.

Okay Okay Okay
Okay Okay
Okay

Sorry
Sorry
Sorry
Sorry
Sorry

Okay Okay

I mean

Congratulations

I mean

I'm
Sorry

It's

Okay

And Beyond

I look down a lot because my neck and
my back are both fused, making
my back my shoulders
and neck hurt
and hard to
look up
and
cannot
glance over my shoulder
or turn most ways,
but I try
still
to
look up at
the sky
when
the
moon
and stars
are out or during a pretty sunset
when both moon and
sun are showing
at the same
time just
as a
quiet evening's dusks settles,
or I notice the sky
during
a grand

thunder
storm
with
awesome lightning
and the beautiful stormy space
speckled with gray clouds
lovely gray wisps
rolling across
right above
always
just
out of physical touch's reach it seems

I always have loved the night
and the moon more
than the sun

Rainbows are an exception

There's always a good reason
to notice these beings
up in our sky
To remember their meanings
or their purposes
and know
they can always connect
with all of ours

Thinking about
being fused
welded
stuck
together and

yet

in

pieces

Much like my bones being fused
so the stars are fused lights
Permanent powerful
fixtures against
a wall
of
unknown darkness…beautiful

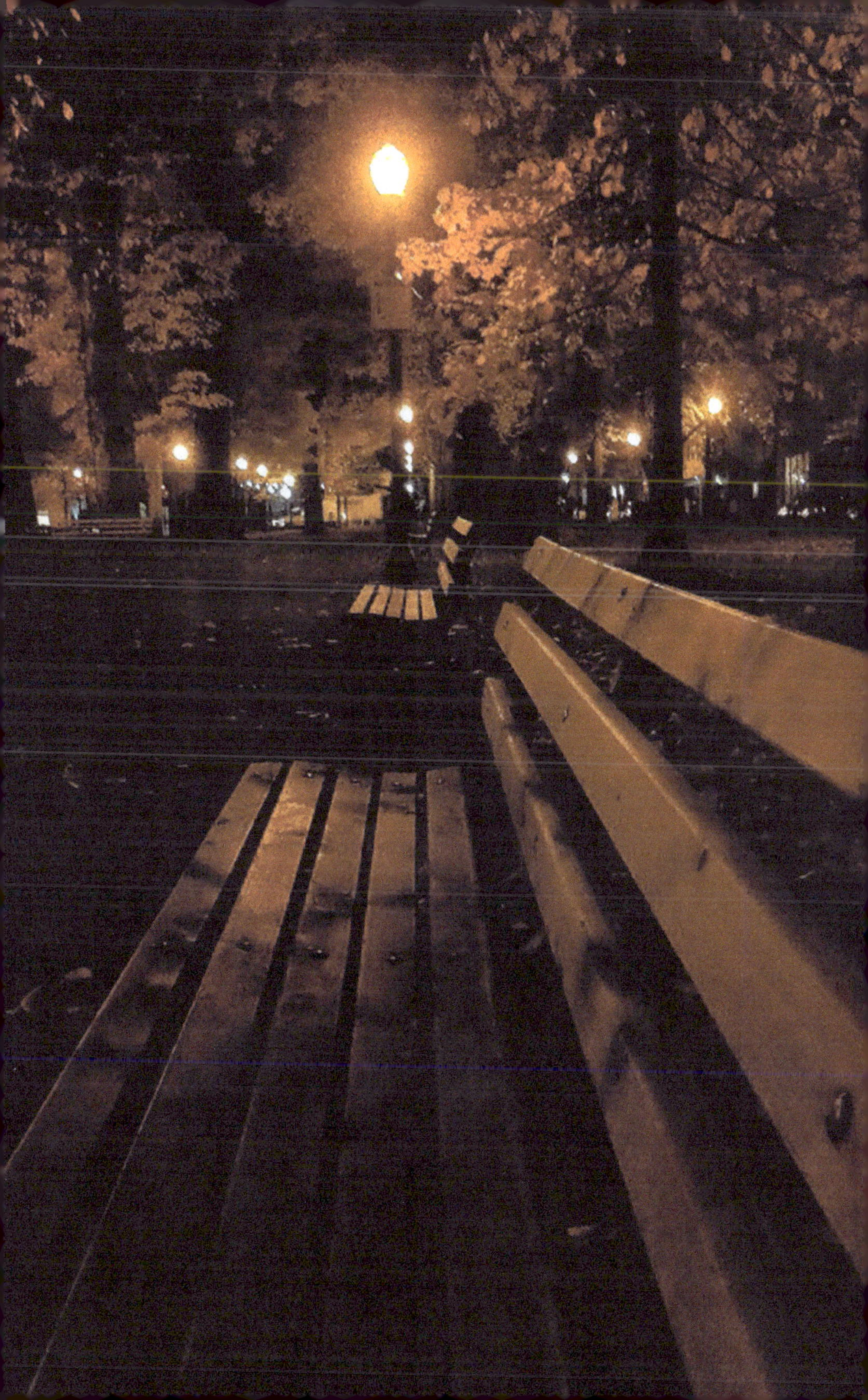

About the Author

Jessica Ann is an aspiring young writer with a beautiful heart for God and yet she possesses a tormented soul, for she has a mission greater than her own pain-stricken life. Jessica was born with a rare chromosome deletion called Velocardiofacial syndrome. This small missing piece inside has afflicted her emotionally, mentally, and physically. Right away, doctors saw her scoliosis and submucous cleft palate for which she had corrective surgeries as they progressed. On the day of her spinal fusion surgery, Jessica's curve had grown to 70 degrees. Prior to surgery, she had been continuously fitted and refitted with back braces. Not to mention her neck having also been partially fused from birth—this trial resulting in having all but one vertebra completely fused, and two metal rods put in her back—but Jessica still knew ever since she was five years old how she possessed a special gift of writing poetry. This gift could only have been explained as God given, because later as a young adult in her late twenties, Jessica would not only suffer from kidney stones but would be diagnosed with fibromyalgia along with the discovery of her chromosome deletion. Everything diagnosed and hidden still is now known to derive from this chromosome deletion or this catch 22; as it is nicknamed figuratively and literally, to get diagnosed with, Jessica still sees her problems as more to write about!

Jessica also survived a private Christian college prep uniformed high school where she was the most misunderstood and most times largely underestimated. Her high school English teacher even called her stupid, but Jessica kept at it. After high school, Jessica waited for college, but she moved with her family to Portland, Oregon, and they found the best apartment location possible to make the going easiest. Moving to Portland was not only to help Jessica, but living there has and still provides the best living, loving and learning accommodations. Not only did Jessica Ann graduate college at Portland State University, despite being diagnosed with something every term, she proved that high school English teacher wrong by making English her major and Writing her minor! (She made As and Bs on most assignments.)

Jessica has always kept writing, no matter what. The poetry flowed out of her as she spilled ink, and this spilled ink became her adopted native name. Jessica's Shawnee heritage connects more pieces of the big picture she frames as a humble Christian servant, striving to stay good and positive through this life we share. Jessica knows this world is not her true home, and this along with proving a few doubtful people wrong fuel her spirit. Now at age forty, Jessica feels it is time to reach more people through her poetry. It is an outlet, but it is so much more while she perseveres in her mission to bring visibility if not compassion from greater understanding for those with illnesses like scoliosis and fibromyalgia that are not as detectable by the human eye. The chromosome deletion Jessica has also needs a spotlight shown in mainstream society. Most people who have this condition never understand even the concept of writing as a verb, much less the gift or talents prevalent in this field. Jessica knows no better way to help others than by sharing her God-given gift. Jessica will keep on having more health obstacles—such as arthritis and restricted lung disease and a tremor in her hands—because of the chromosome deletion. As it connects her health problems altogether, Jessica likes to think of people being connected and how things that seem so very different from each other have very important roles in life that make them connect and relate.